LIFE IS CHANGING FOR:

_____

INTRODUCTION

Taking the time to reflect on life's blessings is crucial for both your mental and physical health. This journal was not created by that of a doctor, but by someone who understands the suffering that comes from anxiety and depression. For the creator, documenting life's blessings has proven to reduce stress, promote healthy sleep patterns, and help achieve overall happiness.

Blessings are everywhere, but as humans, we tend to focus on the concerning, less appealing parts of our lives. Let's shift that focus from what should be, what could be, or even what has been and let's focus on what is and what will be. Life is full of reasons to smile!

Please find time, either first thing in the morning, in the midst of chaos, or at the end of the day (Or all of the above) to reflect on what brings you happiness. Draw attention to even the smallest of life's blessings...When you truly look, they are everywhere! See how your outlook changes and your self-compassion and worth begin to rise.

Happy Changing!

Date:

What are you grateful for?

Date:

What are you grateful for?

Date:

What are you grateful for?

Date:

What are you grateful for?

Date:

What are you grateful for?

Date:

What are you grateful for?

Date:

What are you grateful for?

Date:

What are you grateful for?

Date:

What are you grateful for?

Date:

What are you grateful for?

Date:

What are you grateful for?

Date:

What are you grateful for?

Date:

What are you grateful for?

Date:

What are you grateful for?

Date:

What are you grateful for?

Date:

What are you grateful for?

Date:

What are you grateful for?

Date:

What are you grateful for?

Date:

What are you grateful for?

Date:

What are you grateful for?

Date:

What are you grateful for?

Date:

What are you grateful for?

Date:

What are you grateful for?

Date:

What are you grateful for?

Date:

What are you grateful for?

Date:

What are you grateful for?

Date:

What are you grateful for?

Date:

What are you grateful for?

Date:

What are you grateful for?

Date:

What are you grateful for?

Date:

What are you grateful for?

Date:

What are you grateful for?

Date:

What are you grateful for?

Date:

What are you grateful for?

Date:

What are you grateful for?

Date:

What are you grateful for?

Date:

What are you grateful for?

Date:

What are you grateful for?

Date:

What are you grateful for?

Date:

What are you grateful for?

Date:

What are you grateful for?

Date:

What are you grateful for?

Date:

What are you grateful for?

Date:

What are you grateful for?

Date:

What are you grateful for?

Date:

What are you grateful for?

Date:

What are you grateful for?

Date:

What are you grateful for?

Date:

What are you grateful for?

Date:

What are you grateful for?

Date:

What are you grateful for?

Date:

What are you grateful for?

Date:

What are you grateful for?

Date:

What are you grateful for?

Date:

What are you grateful for?

Date:

What are you grateful for?

Date:

What are you grateful for?

Date:

What are you grateful for?

Date:

What are you grateful for?

Date:

What are you grateful for?

Date:

What are you grateful for?

Date:

What are you grateful for?

Date:

What are you grateful for?

Date:

What are you grateful for?

Date:

What are you grateful for?

Date:

What are you grateful for?

Date:

What are you grateful for?

Date:

What are you grateful for?

Date:

What are you grateful for?

Date:

What are you grateful for?

Date:

What are you grateful for?

Date:

What are you grateful for?

Date:

What are you grateful for?

Date:

What are you grateful for?

Date:

What are you grateful for?

Date:

What are you grateful for?

Date:

What are you grateful for?

Date:

What are you grateful for?

Date:

What are you grateful for?

Date:

What are you grateful for?

Date:

What are you grateful for?

Date:

What are you grateful for?

Date:

What are you grateful for?

Date:

What are you grateful for?

Date:

What are you grateful for?

Date:

What are you grateful for?

Date:

What are you grateful for?

Date:

What are you grateful for?

Date:

What are you grateful for?

Date:

What are you grateful for?

Date:

What are you grateful for?

Date:

What are you grateful for?

Date:

What are you grateful for?

Date:

What are you grateful for?

Date:

What are you grateful for?

Date:

What are you grateful for?

Date:

What are you grateful for?

Date:

What are you grateful for?

Date:

What are you grateful for?

Date:

What are you grateful for?

Date:

What are you grateful for?

Date:

What are you grateful for?

Date:

What are you grateful for?

Date:

What are you grateful for?

Date:

What are you grateful for?

Date:

What are you grateful for?

Date:

What are you grateful for?

Date:

What are you grateful for?

Date:

What are you grateful for?

Date:

What are you grateful for?

Date:

What are you grateful for?

Date:

What are you grateful for?

Date:

What are you grateful for?

Date:

What are you grateful for?

Date:

What are you grateful for?

Date:

What are you grateful for?

Date:

What are you grateful for?

Made in the USA
Las Vegas, NV
15 February 2023